GOOD WORD SERIES

First Family Tree

BIBLE STUDY JOURNAL
ON THE BOOK OF GENESIS

KEVIN STIRRATT

David C. Cook Publishing Co.
Elgin, Illinois/Paris, Ontario

GREAT GROUPS
The Good Word Series
First Family Tree Bible Study Journal
© 1994 David C. Cook Publishing Co.

Published by David C. Cook Publishing Co.
850 North Grove Ave., Elgin, IL 60120
Cable address: DCCOOK
Series editor: Lorraine Triggs. Author: Kevin Stirratt
Designer: Jeff Sharption, PAZ Design Group. Cover illustrator: Ken Cuffe.
Inside illustrator: Bruce Day. Printed in U.S.A. ISBN: 0-7814-5131-0

TABLE OF Contents

How to Do This Bible Study

The three main words of this Bible study are observation, interpretation, and application. You begin with the Bible and discover what's there, dig into the passage to find out what it means, and then apply God's truths to people in general and to you specifically. This kind of Bible study is called inductive study.

Actually, this Bible study is a partially guided inductive study. We'll give some questions to help you with your observations and discoveries. You'll also get some practice in different Bible study methods. You'll be using the overview method as you go through the Book of Genesis. In an overview, you're not looking for nitty-gritty details, but for highlights and major themes. In other words, you'll be looking at the big picture.

Here are the basics you need to know for doing this Bible study.

• Always start with the Scripture passage. Read the entire passage through without stopping. If you look at the Scripture passages printed in this journal, you'll notice that the verses have been left out, and there aren't any headings for the text. That's because you're going to create your own divisions and headings.

• To find out what the passage says, ask the five Ws and one H questions of journalism—who, what, where, when, why, and how. You'll see these questions in various forms throughout the Bible study journal.

• Specific Scripture portions are printed for you in the journal. You'll also need a Bible.

• In the overview method, you're the one who marks the text for reoccurring themes, relationships, events, and insights. Plan on marking up the text that's printed in your journal. That's what it's there for!

• Mark down your observations about the text. As you look at key phrases and relationships, ask yourself what these things tell you about God, people, the relationship between God and people, and the relationship between people and people.

- When you're marking the Scripture for the different themes, characters, and relationships, here are some symbols you could use. Or you can come up with others that would be easier for you to remember. Keep a look out for other symbols that will be suggested throughout these lessons.

☐ People

▲ God

☆ Relationship Between God and People

◼ Relationship Between People and People

● Other Themes

▽ Main Characters

Where It All Began

Genesis 1—4:1-16; 6:5-14

As soon as you open the Bible you are brought face to face with the beginning. In fact, the first four words take us as far back in history as we can go: "In the beginning God. . . ." It all begins with God. Genesis brings us face to face with the amazing power of God. He simply spoke and things came into existence.

The author of the Book of Genesis also shows us a beautiful picture of the beginning of people's relationship with God. But things got a little rough after the Creation. Adam and Eve (the first human beings) rebelled against God when they chose to disobey Him. From that point on, the journey back to God began for all of humanity. It soon becomes obvious that returning to God isn't automatic, but that doesn't mean that God gave up on humanity.

WEEK 1

Let It Be

GENESIS 1:1—2:3

In three to four sentences, describe your neighborhood and what you like and dislike about it.

If you could say the word and make the place you live the way you would want it, what would it be like? Either describe or draw this perfect place of yours.

The amazing thing about Creation is that God just spoke things into existence. He called the shots on what this place and people would be like. Read the Creation account in Genesis as you get ready to explore the power of God in creating everything.

Read all of Genesis 1:1—2:2.

In the beginning God created the heavens and the earth. Now the earth was formless and empty, darkness was over the surface of the deep, and the Spirit of God was hovering over the waters.

And God said, "Let there be light," and there was light. God saw that the light was good, and he separated the light from the darkness. God called the light "day," and the darkness he called "night." And there was evening, and there was morning—the first day.

And God said, "Let there be an expanse between the waters to separate water from water." So God made the expanse and separated the water under the expanse from the water above it. And it was so. God called the expanse "sky." And there was evening, and there was morning—the second day.

And God said, "Let the water under the sky be gathered to one place, and let dry ground appear." And it was so. God called the dry ground "land," and the gathered waters he called "seas." And God saw that it was good.

Then God said, "Let the land produce vegetation: seed-bearing plants and trees on the land that bear fruit with seed in it, according to their various kinds." And it was so. The land produced vegetation: plants bearing seed according to their kinds and trees bearing fruit with seed in it according to their kinds. And God saw that it was good. And there was evening, and there was morning—the third day.

And God said, "Let there be lights in the expanse of the sky to separate the day from the night, and let them serve as signs to mark seasons and days and years, and let them be lights in the expanse of the sky to give light on the earth." And it was so. God made two great lights—the greater light to govern the day and the lesser light to govern the night. He also made the stars. God set them in the expanse of the sky to give light on the earth, to govern the day and the night, and to separate light from darkness. And God saw that it was good. And there was evening, and there was morning—the fourth day.

And God said, "Let the waters teem with living creatures, and let birds fly above the earth across the expanse of the sky." So God created the great creatures of the sea and every living and moving thing with which the water teems, according to their kinds, and every winged bird according to its kind. And God saw that it was good. God blessed them and said, "Be fruitful and increase in number and fill the water in the seas, and let the birds increase on the earth." And there was evening, and there was morning—the fifth day.

And God said, "Let the land produce living creatures according to their kinds: livestock, creatures that move along the ground, and wild animals, each according to its kind." And it was so. God made the wild animals according to their kinds, the livestock according to their kinds, and all the creatures that move along the ground according to their kinds. And God saw that it was good.

Then God said, "Let us make man in our image, in our likeness, and let them rule over the fish of the sea and the birds of the air, over the livestock, over all the earth, and over all the creatures that move along the ground."

So God created man in his own image, in the image of God he created him; male and female he created them.

God blessed them and said to them, "Be fruitful and increase in number; fill the earth and subdue it. Rule over the fish of the sea and the birds of the air and over every living creature that moves on the ground."

Then God said, "I give you every seed-bearing plant on the face of the whole earth and every tree that has fruit with seed in it. They will be yours for food. And to all the beasts of the earth and all the birds of the air and all the creatures that move on the ground—everything that has the breath of life in it—I give every green plant for food." And it was so.

God saw all that he had made, and it was very good. And there was evening, and there was morning—the sixth day.

Thus the heavens and the earth were completed in all their vast array. By the seventh day God had finished the work he had been doing; so on the seventh day he rested from all his work.

1. In a creative way, express the sights, sounds, and smells of the newly created world.

2. Divide the text into sections or scenes. Next, name the scenes, and then write the scene titles in order on the continuum below.

God _____ People

3. Circle the phrase that always marks the end of the "days" of creation. Compare God's view of creation with the way people view creation today.

4. What do you discover about God and His power in Genesis 1?

5. List the differences between Adam's creation and the way everything else was created. What does this tell you about people's role in creation?

6. Write a sentence-summary of Genesis 1:1—2:2.

7. Now that you've broken down the text, what did you learn

about God?

about human beings?

about creation?

about God and people?

8. What does it mean that you're created in God's image?

9. If people really believed that, how would life be different?

PRAYER
PERSONAL

I have hidden your word in my heart that I might not sin against you. Praise be to you, O Lord; teach me your decrees. Psalm 119:11, 12

This page is devoted to your personal conversations with God. Prayer is a two-way conversation. We hear from God through His Word and His Spirit. You can thank Him for what He has taught you and ask for help to put His word into action. By writing down these conversations you can look back and see how you've grown closer to God in the past days. Use the open-ended sentence below to help you get started.

Lord, as I think about Your work of creation, I want to thank You for . . .

Good Help Is Hard to Find

GENESIS 2:4-25

Genesis 2 describes the care God took in placing man in just the right setting with just the right companion. God wanted Adam to have the best person to suit him. Before we look at the care God took in this process, write down the qualities you believe a man or woman needs in order to be a great spouse.

MAN   WOMAN

Read the following portions of Genesis 2.

This is the account of the heavens and the earth when they were created.

When the Lord God made the earth and the heavens—and no shrub of the field had yet appeared on the earth and no plant of the field had yet sprung up, for the Lord God had not sent rain on the earth and there was no man to work the ground, but streams came up from the earth and watered the whole surface of the ground—the Lord God formed the man from the dust of the ground and breathed into his nostrils the breath of life, and the man became a living being.

Now the Lord God had planted a garden in the east, in Eden; and there he put the man he had formed. And the Lord God made all kinds of trees grow out of the ground—trees that were pleasing to the eye and good for food. In the middle of the garden were the tree of life and the tree of the knowledge of good and evil. . . .

The Lord God took the man and put him in the Garden of Eden to work it and take care of it. And the Lord God commanded the man, "You are free to eat from any tree in the garden; but you must not eat from the tree of the knowledge of good and evil, for when you eat of it you will surely die."

The Lord God said, "It is not good for the man to be alone. I will make a helper suitable for him."

Now the Lord God had formed out of the ground all the beasts of the field and all the birds of the air. He brought them to the man to see what he would name them; and whatever the man called each living creature, that was its name. So the man gave names to all the livestock, the birds of the air and all the beasts of the field.

But for Adam no suitable helper was found. So the Lord God caused the man to fall into a deep sleep; and while he was sleeping, he took one of the man's ribs and closed up the place with flesh. Then the Lord God made a woman from the rib he had taken out of the man, and he brought her to the man.

The man said, "This is now bone of my bones and flesh of my flesh; she shall be called 'woman,' for she was taken out of man." For this reason a man will leave his father and mother and be united to his wife, and they will become one flesh.

The man and his wife were both naked, and they felt no shame.

1. Imagine you're sitting in that garden. Describe the sights, sounds, and smells. What's the most important thing in the garden and why?

2. Divide the text into sections. Put a horizontal line at the points you think a new section begins. Now, title the sections, based on their content.

3. If you want to, use the symbols from "How to Do This Bible Study" (page 6), or ones of your own, and mark the different characters in the text. (Yes, God can be one of the characters.) Write their names in the space below. What roles do the characters play?

4. Underline key phrases in the text. (Key phrases are ones that are used consistently in the story.) What do you think is the significance of these key phrases?

5. Go back through the text and put a symbol (see the "How to Do This Bible Study" section again for ones you could use) next to any character or phrase that tells you something about people, God, the relationship between God and people, and the relationship between people and people. Record what you've discovered on the chart below.

God	God—People	People—People

6. What are the differences between the way God created humans and the animals? Between the way God relates to people and the animals?

7. What differences are there between the way Adam relates to God and the way he relates to the animals? Between the way Adam relates to the animals and the way he relates to Eve?

8. Toward the end of the chapter Adam is introduced to his new wife. If you had been in Adam's shoes—assuming Adam wore shoes—how would you have reacted to Eve?

9. Look at the things you discovered about the relationship between God and in this case, man and woman. Do you think there any connections between a person's accountability to God and a person's accountability to his or her spouse? Explain your answer.

10. Based on what you've discovered about the relationship between God and people, as well as man and woman, what are some ways you could show respect for these special relationships?

PRAYER PERSONAL

How many are your works, O Lord! In wisdom you made them all; the earth is full of your creatures. Psalm 104:24

This page is for your personal conversations with God. Begin your conversation with honesty. In the space below confess to God where your relationship to Him and to His creation—fellow man or woman—needs to become more like His original design.

Lord, this is what my relationship to You and others looks like right now . . .

Here's how I want my relationship with You and others to deepen . . .

Lord, this week help me to . . .

WEEK 3
The Buck Stops Here!
GENESIS 3

We've all had to face the reality that we're not perfect. Circle the two situations that would be the hardest for you to face if you were to do them, and then explain why.

Flunking a semester exam

Not living up to my potential

Cheating on a girlfriend or boyfriend

Lying to cover up my tracks

Getting a divorce (assuming I got married)

Shoplifting

Refusing to stand up for a principle I believe in

Betraying a friend's confidence

Other _____

Perfect place. Perfect environment. Perfect people. What could go wrong? A lot—especially when Adam and Eve gave in to temptation. Genesis 3 describes their choice to disobey God and their attempt to pass the buck for their disobedience.

Read all of Genesis 3.

Now the serpent was more crafty than any
of the wild animals the Lord God had
made. He said to the woman, "Did God
really say, 'You must not eat from any tree
in the garden'?"

The woman said to the serpent, "We may
eat fruit from the trees in the garden, but
God did say, 'You must not eat fruit from the tree that is in the middle of the
garden, and you must not touch it, or you will die.' "

"You will not surely die," the serpent said to the woman. "For God knows that
when you eat of it your eyes will be opened, and you will be like God, knowing
good and evil."

When the woman saw that the fruit of the tree was good for food and pleasing
to the eye, and also desirable for gaining wisdom, she took some and ate it. She
also gave some to her husband, who was with her, and he ate it. Then the eyes
of both of them were opened, and they realized they were naked; so they sewed
fig leaves together and made coverings for themselves.

Then the man and his wife heard the sound of the Lord God as he was walking
in the garden in the cool of the day, and they hid from the Lord God among
the trees of the garden. But the Lord God called to the man, "Where are you?"

He answered, "I heard you in the garden, and I was afraid because I was
naked; so I hid."

And he said, "Who told you that you were naked? Have you eaten from the
tree that I commanded you not to eat from?"

The man said, "The woman you put here with me—she gave me some fruit
from the tree, and I ate it."

Then the Lord God said to the woman, "What is this you have done?"

The woman said, "The serpent deceived me, and I ate."

So the Lord God said to the serpent, "Because you have done this, Cursed are you above all the livestock and all the wild animals! You will crawl on your belly and you will eat dust all the days of your life. And I will put enmity between you and the woman, and between your offspring and hers; he will crush your head, and you will strike his heel."

To the woman he said, "I will greatly increase your pains in childbearing; with pain you will give birth to children. Your desire will be for your husband, and he will rule over you."

To Adam he said, "Because you listened to your wife and ate from the tree about which I commanded you, 'You must not eat of it,' Cursed is the ground because of you; through painful toil you will eat of it all the days of your life. It will produce thorns and thistles for you, and you will eat the plants of the field. By the sweat of your brow you will eat your food until you return to the ground, since from it you were taken; for dust you are and to dust you will return."

Adam named his wife Eve, because she would become the mother of all the living.

The Lord God made garments of skin for Adam and his wife and clothed them. And the Lord God said, "The man has now become like one of us, knowing good and evil. He must not be allowed to reach out his hand and take also from the tree of life and eat, and live forever." So the Lord God banished him from the Garden of Eden to work the ground from which he had been taken. After he drove the man out, he placed on the east side of the Garden of Eden cherubim and a flaming sword flashing back and forth to guard the way to the tree of life.

1. Reread the text. What appears to be the author's purpose for writing the text? What do you think he was trying to explain?

2. Divide the text into sections. Think up a movie-like title for each section, based on what happened in it. (For example, the first five sentences could be called, "All About Eve.")

3. List the different characters and their roles. Pay attention to who tempts who and how he or she is tempted. Circle any phrases in the Scripture text that give you insight into the characters, and then describe what you discovered about them.

4. In the Scripture text, trace the blame for the sin. Draw an arrow from the person who started passing the blame to where the blame ended up.

5. Next to each character listed below, describe the curse God pronounced on him or her. Are there any curses that apply to more than one individual? If yes, describe it below.

Adam

Eve

Serpent

6. Now that you have analyzed the characters and their roles, use your symbols (see page 6) and mark up the text to show what you've discovered about God, people, the relationship between God and people, the relationship between people and people (in this case, Adam and Eve), and the relationship between people and the tempter (that is the serpent). Use a curvy line to identify the relationship between people and the tempter. List your findings on the chart below.

God	People	God-People	People-People	People-Tempter

7. The serpent said that Adam and Eve wouldn't die if they ate the fruit. He ended up being right—at least for the time being. What do you think could be the meaning of death in this passage?

8. What was the result of Adam and Eve's disobedience? Do you think this was a fair judgment against Adam and Eve? Why or why not?

9. If you were to summarize the lesson Adam and Eve should have learned through all this, what would it be?

10. Describe the significance of Genesis 3.

11. If Satan were to tempt you with something, what would it be? How can you fight temptation?

PRAYER PERSONAL

This is love for God: to obey his commands. And his commands are not burdensome, for everyone born of God overcomes the world. I John 5:3, 4a

This page is for your personal conversation with God. Begin your conversation with honesty. In the space below, confess to God where you're tempted to give in to sin.

Lord, I have a hard time not giving in to this sin (or sins) . . .

Now, take your confession and turn it into a prayer for change.

Lord, this week help me to . . .

Take a minute to look back over the prayers and requests you wrote down. Put a star next to those prayers God has answered. Put a question mark next to the ones He hasn't answered yet. Take a few minutes to thank God for the way He has answered your prayers. Now, pray for patience to trust God with the other situations. (Remember an answer is sometimes no or not yet.)

A Chip Off the Old Block

GENESIS 4:1-16

Like father, like son. Write down the ways you're like your parents. Include more than the physical resemblance. Think about your mannerisms, your attitudes and views, and even your faith.

PRETTY EASY GOING

LIBERAL   DOMOCRATIC BELIEFS

DONT TAKE LIFE TOO SERIOUS

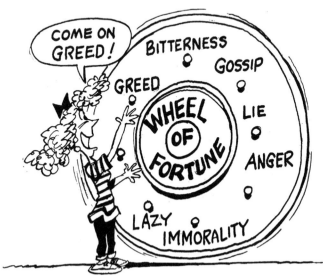

Cain was like his father Adam, especially when it came to giving in to sin. Unfortunately, along with everything else Adam and Eve passed on to the human race, they also passed on sin.

Read Genesis 4:1-16.

Adam lay with his wife Eve, and she became pregnant and gave birth to Cain. She said, "With the help of the Lord I have brought forth a man." Later she gave birth to his brother Abel.

Now Abel kept flocks, and Cain worked the soil. In the course of time Cain brought some of the fruits of the soil as an offering to the Lord. But Abel brought fat portions from some of the firstborn of his flock. The Lord looked with favor on Abel and his offering, but on Cain and his offering he did not look with favor. So Cain was very angry, and his face was downcast.

Then the Lord said to Cain, "Why are you angry? Why is your face downcast? If you do what is right, will you not be accepted? But if you do not do what is right, sin is crouching at your door; it desires to have you, but you must master it."

Now Cain said to his brother Abel, "Let's go out to the field." And while they were in the field, Cain attacked his brother Abel and killed him.

Then the Lord said to Cain, "Where is your brother Abel?"

"I don't know," he replied. "Am I my brother's keeper?"

The Lord said, "What have you done? Listen! Your brother's blood cries out to me from the ground. Now you are under a curse and driven from the ground, which opened its mouth to receive your brother's blood from your hand. When you work the ground, it will no longer yield its crops for you. You will be a restless wanderer on the earth."

Cain said to the Lord, "My punishment is more than I can bear. Today you are driving me from the land, and I will be hidden from your presence; I will be a restless wanderer on the earth, and whoever finds me will kill me."

But the Lord said to him, "Not so; if anyone kills Cain, he will suffer vengeance seven times over." Then the Lord put a mark on Cain so that no one who found him would kill him. So Cain went out from the Lord's presence and lived in the land of Nod, east of Eden.

1. As usual, divide the text into sections, and come up with titles. Also, write a short sentence summary of each section in the margins.

2. Using your symbols, mark the different relationships in the text, and then fill in the chart.

God	People	God—People	People—People

3. How does God describe Cain's temptation to kill his brother? What picture does this description bring to mind? Write or draw that image. What do you discover about the nature of sin?

4. What do you think is the key question of the text? Who asks it? Of whom is it asked? Based on this key question, state the purpose of the text.

5. Identify the steps Cain took that caused him to sin. Check out his motives and attitudes. We've suggested the first and last steps, but feel free to replace them with your own. Don't worry about filling in all the spaces.

• Cain brings an offering to God.

•

•

•

•

•

•

• Cain kills his brother.

6. Describe Cain's emotions. What sin do you think Cain had problems with? Do you think Cain ever faced his sin? Why or why not?

7. Why do you think God didn't wipe Cain out? What does this tell you about God?

8. In what situations are you most likely to be jealous? What can you do about it?

PRAYER
PERSONAL

Submit yourselves, then, to God. Resist the devil, and he will flee from you. Come near to God and he will come near to you. Wash your hands, you sinners, and purify your hearts, you double-minded. Grieve, mourn and wail. Change your laughter to mourning and your joy to gloom. Humble yourselves before the Lord, and he will lift you up. James 4:7-10

Talking honestly with God about your sin is extremely important in a growing relationship with Him. If you try to cover up sin, you'll never be open enough to ask for God's help and forgiveness—two things He freely gives you.

Lord, I don't want cover up my sin, so I confess that I struggle with feelings of jealousy in this situation . . .

Because . . .

I want Your forgiveness, and I need Your help to . . .

Thank You for forgiving me and helping me to live for You.

When Bad Things Happen to Bad People

GENESIS 6:5-14

Write one or two things that can "kill"

a friendship:

your grades:

a reputation:

your relationship with God:

God knew all along that once aware of good and evil, people would die. It didn't happen all at once, but bit by bit a person's constant choice to do wrong would eventually kill him or her. At this point in Genesis, things have gone from bad to worse, and God was ready to take drastic action.

Read all of Genesis 6:5-14.

The Lord saw how great man's wickedness on the earth had become, and that every inclination of the thoughts of his heart was only evil all the time. The Lord was grieved that he had made man on the earth, and his heart was filled with pain. So the Lord said, "I will wipe mankind, whom I have created, from the face of the earth—men and animals, and creatures that move along the ground, and birds of the air—for I am grieved that I have made them." But Noah found favor in the eyes of the Lord.

This is the account of Noah.

Noah was a righteous man, blameless among the people of his time, and he walked with God. Noah had three sons: Shem, Ham and Japheth.

Now the earth was corrupt in God's sight and was full of violence. God saw how corrupt the earth had become, for all the people on earth had corrupted their ways. So God said to Noah, "I am going to put an end to all people, for the earth is filled with violence because of them. I am surely going to destroy both them and the earth. So make yourself an ark of cypress wood; make rooms in it and coat it with pitch inside and out."

1. Think of a title for this passage, and write it above the verses. Why did you pick that title?

2. Put a question mark next to anything in the text you have questions about or problems with.

3. Now, underline any phrases or sentences you feel provide insight to the story line. How do these sentences explain what's going on?

4. In the chart try to identify the situations people created for themselves and God's response to the situation. In the third column, describe what you think was going on in God's mind. (Look for clues in the passage.)

The Situation	God's Response	God's Mind

5. List Noah's character traits. Also, look up Genesis 6:22 in your Bible for one more trait.

6. Even though nothing is said in the Bible, you've got to believe that Noah had major conflicts with the people around him. What do you think other people may have said about Noah, especially after he started to build that ark?

7. On what did God base His decision to wipe out humanity and creation? How do you think people today are doing in God's eyes? Give reasons or examples for your answer.

8. Write down some of the things you discovered about God and His attitude toward sin. Let's get a little personal now. What's your attitude toward sin?

9. Ever since sin came on the scene, people have had a natural bent toward evil. What are some ways people try to cope with this natural bent? What do you think is the best way?

Not that I have already obtained all this, or have already been made perfect, but I press on to take hold of that for which Christ Jesus took hold of me. Brothers, I do not consider myself yet to have taken hold of it. But one thing I do: Forgetting what is behind and straining toward what is ahead, I press on toward the goal to win the prize for which God has called me heavenward in Christ Jesus. Philippians 3:12-14

Sin is serious business. You can come to God, however, and confess your sins and thank Him for His forgiveness. Be sure to include both when you pray. As you confess your sins, you'll find the freedom to grow in your relationship to God.

Finish this prayer, and then pray it back to God.

Lord, I confess my sins to You. Lately I've been struggling to . . .

Lord, You give me hope. When I feel like I've failed beyond the point of no return, You help me to . . .

Lord, I want to live for You, help me . . .

Thank You for forgiving me and showing me how to live for You. In Jesus' name. Amen.

Somewhere Under the Rainbow

Genesis 6:17—9:17; 11—12:9; 15; 17; 21

By the time you get to Genesis 6, sin has taken its toll. You see, Adam and Eve committed a real sin that had real consequences for the rest of humanity. People were so affected by sin that they were doing evil all the time—except for one family and one person who had a right relationship with God. So God took action, drastic action, in dealing with sin. Some people have problems with the way God handled the situation, but God's actions reflected the seriousness of sin.

After you read about a flood of catastrophic proportions, a rainbow, and a tower in Genesis 6-11, you'll discover that God chooses to work with people as they are—sinful. You'll also learn about the new relationship people have with God under the rainbow, under God's promise of patience and kindness.

WEEK 6

Going to Extremes

GENESIS 6:17— 7:11, 17—8:1-5

A lot of people go to extremes with God. He's either all hell, fire, and brimstone, or all sweetness and light. The truth is that God isn't all one way or the other. He doesn't fit into any boxes people try to create for Him. As His creations, we need to learn how to live with His perfect paradoxes.

I'm uncomfortable with (circle all that apply):

• God's judgment.

• God's seeming silence.

• God's demands for holiness and obedience.

• God's timetable for bringing about justice.

• Other _____ .

When we last left Noah, he was building an ark of cypress wood and coating it with pitch. Now, Noah and his family are about to enter the ark . . . with two of every kind of bird and animal. Talk about going to extremes in obeying God.

Read the following portions of Genesis 6:17—7:11, 17—8:1-5.

"I am going to bring floodwaters on the earth to destroy all life under the heavens, every creature that has the breath of life in it. Everything on earth will perish. But I will establish my covenant with you, and you will enter the ark—you and your sons and your wife and your sons' wives with you. . . ."

Noah did everything just as God commanded him.

The Lord then said to Noah, "Go into the ark, you and your whole family, because I have found you righteous in this generation. Take with you seven of every kind of clean animal, a male and its mate, and two of every kind of unclean animal, a male and its mate, and also seven of every kind of bird, male and female, to keep their various kinds alive throughout the earth. Seven days from now I will  send rain on the earth for forty days and forty nights, and I will wipe from the face of the earth every living creature I have made."

And Noah did all that the Lord commanded him. . . .

For forty days the flood kept coming on the earth, and as the waters increased they lifted the ark high above the earth. The waters rose and increased greatly on the earth, and the ark floated on the surface of the water. Every living thing on the face of the earth was wiped out; men and animals and the creatures that move along the ground and the birds of the air were wiped from the earth. Only Noah was left, and those with him in the ark. . . .

But God remembered Noah and all the wild animals and the livestock that were with him in the ark, and he sent a wind over the earth, and the waters receded. Now the springs of the deep and the floodgates of the heavens had been closed, and the rain had stopped falling from the sky. The water receded steadily from the earth. At the end of the hundred and fifty days the water had gone down, and on the seventeenth day of the seventh month the ark came to rest on the mountains of Ararat. The waters continued to recede until the tenth month, and the first day of the tenth month the tops of the mountains became visible.

1. Go through the passage and list as many details as you can about these things. Also, check out Genesis 6 and 7 in your Bibles for more details.

• the ark

• God's decision

• the animals

• the Flood itself

2. Underline any repeated phrases or sentences in the passage. What do you think is the significance of these phrases?

3. In one to three sentences summarize the passage. Ask the who, what, when, where, why, how, and so what questions.

4. Reread the first paragraph of the Scripture text. In one breath, God is wiping out everything and everyone; and in the next He's making a promise to Noah. Write down some of your thoughts and feelings about this. Is God being fair? He is purposely playing favorites?

5. From the way God related to Noah, what can you discover about God?

6. Other than a flood, what are some other ways God could get the attention of the world today? What do you think He would say or do to focus attention—and obedience—on His commands?

7. Write down any questions or problems you have with this study. Also, write down the one truth that hit you.

8. Noah's story is all about obedience to God. Finish these sentences.

• For me, obeying God means . . .

• It's easy for me to obey God when . . .

• It's hard for me to obey God when . . .

PRAYER
PERSONAL

I lift up my eyes to the hills—where does my help come from? My help comes from the Lord, the Maker of heaven and earth. Psalm 121:1, 2

A relationship with God will always be filled with things that may not make sense from a human perspective. One of these paradoxes is that the very God, the maker of heaven and earth, who demands our obedience is also the one who will help us obey Him . . . and forgive us when we sin.

Finish this prayer.

God, here are some things that still don't make sense about You:

Even though I don't understand everything, I want to obey You. Help me obey You in this particular situation . . .

Thank You for Your help, and for Your forgiveness. In Jesus' name. Amen.

Never Again

GENESIS 8:13—9:3, 8-17

Without being really serious, think about a time you were in the middle of something and it suddenly dawned on that you'd never do this again. Describe the situation, and how you got roped into it.

The Flood was over, and everything was wiped out. God then made a promise that He would never again destroy all earthly life by a natural catastrophe. This promise was signed, sealed, and delivered by God Himself.

Read the folowing portions of Genesis 8:13—9:3, 8-17

By the first day of the first month of Noah's six hundred and first year, the water had dried up from the earth. Noah then removed the covering from the ark and saw that the surface of the ground was dry. By the twenty-seventh day of the second month the earth was completely dry.

Then God said to Noah, "Come out of the ark, you and your wife and your sons and their wives. Bring out every kind of living creature that is with you—the birds, the animals, and all the creatures that move along the

ground—so they can multiply on the earth and be fruitful and increase in number upon it." So Noah came out, together with his sons and his wife and his sons' wives. All the animals and all the creatures that move along the ground and all the birds—everything that moves on the earth—came out of the ark, one kind after another.

Then Noah built an altar to the Lord and, taking some of all the clean animals and clean birds, he sacrificed burnt offerings on it. The Lord smelled the pleasing aroma and said in his heart: "Never again will I curse the ground because of man, even though every inclination of his heart is evil from childhood. And never again will I destroy all living creatures, as I have done. ·

"As long as the earth endures, seedtime and harvest, cold and heat, summer and winter, day and night will never cease."

Then God blessed Noah and his sons, saying to them, "Be fruitful and increase in number and fill the earth. The fear and dread of you will fall upon all the beasts of the earth and all the birds of the air, upon every creature that moves along the ground, and upon all the fish of the sea; they are given into your hands. Everything that lives and moves will be food for you. Just as I gave you the green plants, I now give you everything. . . ."

Then God said to Noah and to his sons with him: "I now establish my covenant with you and with your descendants after you and with every living creature that was with you—the birds, the livestock and all the wild animals, all those that came out of the ark with you—every living creature on earth. I establish my covenant with you: Never again will all life be cut off by the waters of a flood; never again will there be a flood to destroy the earth."

And God said, "This is the sign of the covenant I am making between me and you and every living creature with you, a covenant for all generations to come: I have set my rainbow in the clouds, and it will be the sign of the covenant between me and the earth. Whenever I bring clouds over the earth and the rainbow appears in the clouds, I will remember my covenant between me and you and all living creatures of every kind. Never again will the waters become a flood to destroy all life. Whenever the rainbow appears in the clouds, I will see it and remember the everlasting covenant between God and all living creatures of every kind on the earth."

So God said to Noah, "This is the sign of the covenant I have established between me and all life on the earth."

1. Just for the fun of it, write down what you think was Noah's first comment when he was finally out of the ark.

2. Underline any phrases or sentences in the passage that you think give insight to the story line. What do those sentences talk about? Explain your choices.

3. In your Bible, skim Genesis 6 and 7. On the chart below, describe humanity before the Flood and God's response. In the "after" column, describe God's response to Noah after the Flood, based on this week's text. In the final column, write some reasons for God's change of heart.

Before the Flood	After the Flood	Change of heart

4. Now, go back through the text and identify the themes you see, and then record your observations on the chart.

God	People	God—People	People—People

5. Using the chart in question four, write down anything that's new or different in God's relationship with people.

6. Take a closer look at the promise God made to Noah.

• Who did God make it with?

• Describe the promise.

• Describe the sign God gave.

7. Look at the command God gave Noah and his sons after He promised never to destroy the earth through a flood. Sound familiar? Who else did God tell this to in the Book of Genesis? Explain the role Noah and his family had in God's plan.

8. Reread the section with that famous rainbow. Describe how you feel when you see a rainbow. What does this tell you about God's character?

9. Circle all the times the word "remember" pops up in the text. Why do you think this is such a big deal to God?

10. Skim through your Bible, and write down any promises God makes that you can claim for yourself. What do these promises mean to you?

PRAYER
PERSONAL

Therefore let everyone who is godly pray to you while you may be found; surely when the mighty waters rise, they will not reach him. You are my hiding place; you will protect me from trouble and surround me with songs of deliverance.
Psalm 32:6, 7

Thank God for the things He has shown you in His Word. Praise Him for the way He helps you. Make a commitment to put into action what you have learned from His Word.

Lord, thank You for showing me these things in Your Word this week:

Thank You for the times you have helped me. (List any times you can think of here.)

I am going to put Your Word into action this week by . . .

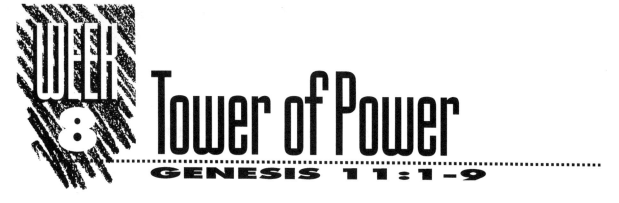

WEEK 8

Tower of Power

GENESIS 11:1-9

VICTIMS OF MALLNESIA

Sniglets are handy word devices that help you avoid long, boring detailed descriptions. You know that fake green grass that goes in Easter baskets? Its sniglet is "Eastro turf". Or when you go to the mall, and then forget why you came, you're suffering from mallnesia. Get it? Think up a sniglet or two of your own.

In some ways, if you have information and communication, you have power. And there's nothing wrong with a little control and ambition. After all, everyone wants to get ahead. But what happens when you get so far ahead that you end up competing with God?

Read all of Genesis 11:1-9.

Now the whole world had one language and a common speech. As men moved eastward, they found a plain in Shinar and settled there.

They said to each other, "Come, let's make bricks and bake them thoroughly." They used brick instead of stone, and tar for mortar. Then they said, "Come, let us build ourselves a city, with a tower that reaches to the heavens, so that we may make a name for ourselves and not be scattered over the face of the whole earth."

But the Lord came down to see the city and the tower that the men were building. The Lord said, "If as one people speaking the same language they have begun to do this, then nothing they plan to do will be impossible for them. Come, let us go down and confuse their language so they will not understand each other."

So the Lord scattered them from there over all the earth, and they stopped building the city. That is why it was called Babel—because there the Lord confused the language of the whole world. From there the Lord scattered them over the face of the whole earth.

1. Divide this short passage into scenes, and write down your observations. Pay attention to the details in each scene.

2. Circle any repeated words or phrases that you think are significant, and explain why you chose them.

3. Write down the two different perspectives on this passage—God's and humanity's.

4. Was God really threatened by the tower? Explain your answer.

5. Why did God want the people scattered? What do you think about the way God handled things?

6. Fill in the chart with what you discovered about these relationships.

God	People	God—People	People—People

7. In your informed, backed-by-the-text opinion, what was these people's main problem?

8. Is there one thing that you just don't get about this passage? If so, put a star next to it in the passage.

9. What are some ways people try to play God

• in business?

• in science?

• in entertainment?

• in academics?

• in law?

PRAYER
PERSONAL

My son, do not make light of the Lord's discipline, and do not lose heart when he rebukes you, because the Lord disciplines those he loves, and he punishes everyone he accepts as a son. Hebrews 12:5, 6

This page is for your personal conversation with God. Even though it's not the most upbeat way to start a conversation, confess your selfish ambition to God. Ask Him to help you to be ambitious for His plans in His way. Commit yourself to putting into action the things you've discovered about God, people, and their relationship with each other.

Lord, I have a tendency to seek my own way, especially when . . .

I confess my sin of . . .

Help me to follow Your plans before my own. I want to give up my desires when they conflict with Your perfect design. Help me in this. It will be hard for me to . . .

Thank You for . . .

WEEK 9 Promises, Promises
GENESIS 11:27— 12:9

What kind of promises do you make?

• Some promises I've made:

• Some promises others have made to me:

• Some promises I'm likely to make in the future:

God's into making promises too. The first thing God gives Abram is a promise. The only problem is that Abram has no idea of how God's going to keep His promise. Abram, however, has some idea of who God is, so he decides to take the risk and trust God.

One more thing, Abram, Abraham—same person. In Genesis 17:5, God reaffirmed His promise to Abram and changed his name to Abraham, which means "father of many." Since this week's study is in chapters 11 and 12 we're using the name Abram.

Read Genesis 11:27—12:9.

This is the account of Terah.

Terah became the father of Abram, Nahor and Haran. And Haran became the father of Lot. While his father Terah was still alive, Haran died in Ur of the Chaldeans, in the land of his birth. Abram and Nahor both married. The name of Abram's wife was Sarai, and the name of Nahor's wife was Milcah; she was the daughter of Haran, the father of both Milcah and Iscah. Now Sarai was barren; she had no children.

Terah took his son Abram, his grandson Lot son of Haran, and his daughter-in-law Sarai, the wife of his son Abram, and together they went out from Ur of the Chaldeans to go to Canaan. But when they came to Haran, they settled there.

Terah lived 205 years, and he died in Haran.

The Lord had said to Abram, "Leave your country, your people and your father's household and go to the land I will show you.

"I will make you into a great nation

and I will bless you;

I will make your name great,

and you will be a blessing.

I will bless those who bless you,

and whoever curses you I will curse;

and all peoples on earth

will be blessed through you."

So Abram left, as the Lord had told him; and Lot went with him. Abram was seventy-five years old when he set out from Haran. He took his wife Sarai, his nephew Lot, all the possessions they had accumulated and the people they had acquired in Haran, and they set out for the land of Canaan, and they arrived there.

Abram traveled through the land as far as the site of the great tree of Moreh at Shechem. At that time the Canaanites were in the land. The Lord appeared to Abram and said, "To your offspring I will give this land." So he built an altar there to the Lord, who had appeared to him.

From there he went on toward the hills east of Bethel and pitched his tent, with Bethel on the west and Ai on the east. There he built an altar to the Lord and called on the name of the Lord. Then Abram set out and continued toward the Negev.

1. Come up with a newspaper headline that you think captures the heart of the story.

2. List each part of God's promise to Abram, and the effect you think it had on Abram.

3. What do you think is the significance of this promise? Do you think Abram actually understood it all? Why or why not?

4. Why did God choose to give this promise to Abram? Look for clues in the text to help with your answer.

5. What do you discover about God from His promise to Abram?

6. Describe Abram's faith and obedience. What assumption do you think Abram was operating on?

7. List everything that Abram had, and what he gave up to follow God. What would you be willing to give up to follow God?

8. Abram had the option either to take God at His word or not. What do you think would be difficult for you about this all-or-nothing kind of faith?

PRAYER PERSONAL

He redeemed us in order that the blessing given to Abraham might come to the Gentiles through Christ Jesus, so that by faith we might receive the promise of the Spirit. Galatians 3:14

It's not easy to trust God when you don't know how things will turn out. It's a matter of wanting to be in control. Complete this prayer, and talk to God about His promises and your desires. Also, commit yourself to following God's will—without preconceived notions or limitations of what it might mean for you.

Lord, sometimes I want something so much that I convince myself that You want it for me too. These are the things I am not sure about . . .

Lord, I have learned in Your Word that You have promised to . . .

Help me trust You with these things in my life . . .

Thank You for keeping Your promises, and thank You for . . .

Believe It

GENESIS 15; 17; 21

Do you think skepticism and cynicism are cool? Or do you believe everything anyone tells you? Check the statement that best describes you.

___ Most trusting soul around

___ If it's in print or on TV, I believe it

___ As long as I know and trust
the source

___ Only if it's a proven fact

___ Major cynic here

Abraham (as he's now called) may have been the most trusting soul around in ancient times. God had made this wild promise, and Abraham believed it, because he knew and trusted the source.

Read Genesis 15:1-6; 17:1-7, 15-17; 21:1-5.

(You'll need your Bible too.)

After this, the word of the Lord came to Abram in a vision: "Do not be afraid, Abram. I am your shield, your very great reward."

But Abram said, "O Sovereign Lord, what can you give me since I remain childless and the one who will inherit my estate is Eliezer of Damascus?" And Abram said, "You have given me no children; so a servant in my household will be my heir."

A TRILLION AND ONE, A TRILLION AND TWO...

Then the word of the Lord came to him: "This man will not be your heir, but a son coming from your own body will be your heir." He took him outside and said, "Look up at the heavens and count the stars—if indeed you can count them." Then he said to him, "So shall your offspring be."

Abram believed the Lord, and he credited it to him as righteousness.

*   *   *

When Abram was ninety-nine years old, the Lord appeared to him and said, "I am God Almighty; walk before me and be blameless. I will confirm my covenant between me and you and will greatly increase your numbers."

Abram fell facedown, and God said to him, "As for me, this is my covenant with you: You will be the father of many nations. No longer will you be called Abram; your name will be Abraham, for I have made you a father of many nations. I will make you very fruitful; I will make nations of you, and kings will come from you. I will establish my covenant as an everlasting covenant between me and you and your descendants after you for the generations to come, to be your God and the God of your descendants after you."

God also said to Abraham, "As for your Sarai your wife, you are no longer to call her Sarai; her name will be Sarah. I will bless her and will surely give you a son by her. I will bless her so that she will be the mother of nations; kings of peoples will come from her."

Abraham fell facedown; he laughed and said to himself, "Will a son be born to a man a hundred years old? Will Sarah bear a child at the age of ninety?"

*   *   *

Now the Lord was gracious to Sarah as he had said, and the Lord did for Sarah what he had promised. Sarah became pregnant and bore a son to Abraham in his old age, at the very time God had promised him. Abraham gave the name Isaac to the son Sarah bore him. When his son Isaac was eight days old, Abraham circumcised him, as God commanded him. Abraham was a hundred years old when his son Isaac was born to him.

1. To get the big picture of what's going on between God and Abraham, skim Genesis 15—21, not just the Scripture that's printed here. When you've finished, fill in the chart.

God	People	God—People	People—People	Other Themes

2. Go back through the text, and mark the different names of God and how He is referred to. Also, look up Genesis 16:13, 14 in your Bible. Write down what you discover about God and His character.

3. Create a biography for Abraham. Include things like family, background, position, and outstanding character traits. You might want to glance through all of Abraham's story, beginning with Genesis 12 and ending with Genesis 21. At the end of your biography, write a short description of Abraham.

4. This is only the fourth time that God repeats His promise to Abraham. (See Genesis 12:1-3; 13:14-16; and 15:4, 5.) Is there anything new in this passage? If so, what? What's the basis of the promise?

5. What do you think is the significance of God's changing the names of Abram and Sarai to Abraham and Sarah? Suppose God gave you a new name.What would you want it to be and why?

6. Go through the text and circle all the emotions that are floating around. How do you think this might have affected Abraham and Sarah?

7. Look up Genesis 12:4 and Genesis 16:16, and also underline any ages mentioned in the text that's printed here. Next, figure out how long it was from the time of the promise and the actual birth of Isaac. What effect do you think this time lapse had on Abraham's and Sarah's faith?

8. Do you think Abraham was a person of faith? Why or why not? (Remember to support your answer from the text. You can include the other chapters too.)

9. Describe how a time lapse affects your faith (or could affect it), especially when it doesn't seem like God is doing anything.

PRAYER PERSONAL

By faith Abraham, even though he was past age—and Sarah herself was barren—was enabled to become a father because he considered him faithful who had made the promise. Hebrews 11:11

As far as Abraham was concerned, it was up to God to keep His promise. You see, once you know who God is, you can trust Him no matter what. He'll always keep His word.

God, right now my level of trust in You is . . .

Because . . .

Help me trust You in this particular situation . . .

And thank You for being trustworthy.

Give me patience, faith, determination, insight, and wisdom in order that I might influence my world for Your sake. In Jesus' name. Amen.

UNIT Three

ABRAHAM, ISAAC, JACOB AND JOSEPH, THIS IS YOUR LIFE !!

The Founding Fathers

Genesis 22—25; 27; 37; 39; 41—45

Romance! Deception! Trickery! Intrigue!

No, we haven't been reading the tabloids again (besides, we only read the headlines), we're just continuing in the Book of Genesis. At this point in the book, we go from talking about gargantuan events and many nations to the very personal and private lives of Abraham, Isaac, Jacob, and Joseph—names that may already be familiar to you. These are the main characters, the founding fathers (patriarchs is the technical term), of God's chosen people.

God chose to bless these founding fathers in big ways. But did God's blessing mean fair treatment? A problem-free existence? A fantastic family life? Amazing wisdom? Actually, no. God's blessing was a promise that He alone would give His people a hope for the future, in all its uncertainty.

We have the same God and the same hope today. And even if that involves heartache, separation, unfair circumstances, unreasonable relationships, or whatever, we can say with Joseph, "God intended it for good. . . ."

The Ultimate "Yes" Man

GENESIS 22:1-19

In the first column, list your five most prized possessions. In the second column, list how long it took you to acquire those things, and in the third column, list their approximate value to you. (The value could be monetary as in the actual bucks you paid for the item, or its sentimental value.)

Prized Possession	Time to Acquire	Approximate Value
1.		
2.		
3.		
4.		
5.		

Now, put a check mark next to the possessions you'd be willing to loan to an extremely close friend, even though your friend wouldn't tell you what he or she was going to do with your stuff.

Guess what? God kept His promise (big surprise), and gave Abraham a son—the promised heir, Isaac. Then God turns

around and wants Abraham to give up his son. Abraham looks like the ultimate "yes" man, because he obeys God, no questions asked.

We're now calling Abram, Abraham. You might want to skim Genesis 16—18 to fill in some background to this week's story.

Read all of Genesis 22:1-19.

Some time later God tested Abraham. He said to him, "Abraham!"

"Here I am," he replied.

Then God said, "Take your son, your only son, Isaac, whom you love, and go to the region of Moriah. Sacrifice him there as a burnt offering on one of the mountains I will tell you about."

Early the next morning Abraham got up and saddled his donkey. He took with him two of his servants and his son Isaac. When he had cut enough wood for the burnt offering, he set out for the place God had told him about. On the third day Abraham looked up and saw the place in the distance. He said to his servants, "Stay here with the donkey while I and the boy go over there. We will worship and then we will come back to you."

Abraham took the wood for the burnt offering and placed it on his son Isaac, and he himself carried the fire and the knife. As the two of them went on together, Isaac spoke up and said to his father Abraham, "Father?"

"Yes, my son?" Abraham replied.

"The fire and wood are here," Isaac said, "but where is the lamb for the burnt offering?"

Abraham answered, "God himself will provide the lamb for the burnt offering, my son." And the two of them went on together.

When they reached the place God had told him about, Abraham built an altar there and arranged the wood on it. He bound his son Isaac and laid him on the altar, on top of the wood. Then he reached out his hand and took the knife to slay his son. But the angel of the Lord called out to him from heaven, "Abraham! Abraham!"

"Here I am," he replied.

"Do not lay a hand on the boy." he said, "Do not do anything to him. Now I know that you fear God, because you have not withheld from me your son, your only son."

Abraham looked up and there in a thicket he saw a ram caught by its horns. He went over and took the ram and sacrificed it as a burnt offering instead of his son. So Abraham called that place The Lord Will Provide. And to this day it is said, "On the mountain of the Lord it will be provided."

The angel of the Lord called to Abraham from heaven a second time and said, "I swear by myself, declares the Lord, that because you have done this and have not withheld your son, your only son, I will surely bless you and make your descendants as numerous as the stars in the sky and as the sand on the seashore. Your descendants will take possession of the cities of their enemies, and through your offspring all nations on earth will be blessed, because you have obeyed me."

Then Abraham returned to his servants, and they set off together for Beersheba. And Abraham stayed in Beersheba.

1. Reread the text, and then come up with a clever title and plug for a TV mini-series about Abraham and Isaac.

2. Go back through the text and mark the main characters. Put an exclamation mark next to anything the characters do that you think is out of character for them. In the space below, write down your reactions to when this happens.

3. Go back through the text and mark these themes you see. (Use the symbols listed on page 6.) Also, mark other themes you see in the passage. Record the themes in the appropriate column on the chart. You may want to add other themes from last week's study to this week's chart. This will help you see the big picture of Abraham's life.

God	People	God—People	People—People	Other Themes

4.Look at the times God and Abraham had a conversation. What do you discover about Abraham's relationship with God? Does this remind you of an earlier conversation in Genesis between God and people? If it does, contrast these two different conversations.

5. In the space below, first write down all the questions that are asked in the passage and who asks them. What questions would you have considered "reasonable" and would have asked if you were in Abraham's place? Fill in the chart with your question, the importance of an answer, and the effect it would have on your faith. Be honest.

"Reasonable" question	Importance of answer	Effect on my faith

6. Investigate the passage for emotions and clues to how Abraham felt about Isaac. What did Abraham stand to lose if he followed God's command? (Get the obvious answer out of the way first.) What insights does this give you into Abraham's level of trust in God?

7. Look at Isaac's question to Abraham as they were walking toward the place of sacrifice. How would you have answered Isaac? What does Abraham's response tell you about Abraham's heart? Do you believe Abraham really believed what he told Isaac? Explain your answer.

8. What's your gut-level reaction to what God is putting Abraham through? Does this fit with your understanding of who God is? Does God really test people this way?

9. Based on this story, list all the things you think are important in a person's relationship with God. Number the items in order of their importance.

10. Abraham had mega-confidence in God. Think about your relationship with God; then check the statement that best describes where you are right now.

___ I don't think I know God well enough to trust Him like that.

___ I would need a lot more answers and explanations before I'd trust God.

___ I'd try to trust God, but my heart might not be in it.

___ I'd trust God even if it wouldn't seem like the logical thing to do.

PRAYER PERSONAL

Let come to me what may. Why do I put myself in jeopardy and take my life in my hands? Though he slay me, yet will I hope in him.—Job 13:13b-15a

It's not always easy trusting God's promise, especially when you haven't the foggiest notion of how things will turn out. It's tempting to rely on things you can see and know for a fact. If you want to follow God, however, your security has to be in Him alone—nothing less and nothing more.

Finish this prayer, and then make a commitment to taking specific steps to answer God with a quiet, quick yes.

Lord, I tend to rely more on things that I can see and prove than on You. I have realized from Your Word that I can trust You because . . .

Help me trust You as I deal with these areas of my life . . .

In the past I have tried to rely on other things for my security. Specifically, I have . . .

But, this week help me act with a deep trust in Your faithfulness to me as I . . .

In-Between Times

GENESIS 24; 25:19-21

Life is is full of transitions, plans, obstacles to plans, and frustrations. For each of the categories listed below, write down some transitions you're experiencing, as well as plans or even obstacles you might have to deal with. Next, think through some ways God might help you.

	Transition	Plans	Obstacles	How God can help
My Faith				
My Home Life				
My Education				
My Future Family				
My Career				

For Abraham, belonging to God's chosen family meant trusting God and His design in those in-between times. As Abraham approaches the end of his life, he makes plans for his son, Isaac, to take center stage in God's plans.

Read the following portions of Genesis 24—25:19-21.

Abraham was now old and well advanced in years, and the Lord had blessed him in every way. He said to the chief servant in his household, the one in charge of all that he had, "Put your hand under my thigh. I want you to swear by the Lord, the God of heaven and the God of earth, that you will not get a wife for my son from the daughters of the Canaanites, among whom I am living, but will go to my country and my own relatives and get a wife for my son Isaac."

The servant asked him, "What if the woman is unwilling to come back with me to this land? Shall I then take your son back to the country you came from?"

"Make sure that you do not take my son back there," Abraham said. "The Lord, the God of heaven, who brought me out of my father's household and my native land and who spoke to me and promised me on oath, saying, 'To your offspring I will give this land'—he will send his angel before you so that you can get a wife for my son from there. If the woman is unwilling to come back with you, then you will be released from this oath of mine. Only do not take my son back there." So the servant put his hand under the thigh of his master Abraham and swore an oath to him concerning this matter. . . .

He set out for Aram Naharaim and made his way to the town of Nahor. He had the camels kneel down near the well outside the town. . . .

Then he prayed, "O Lord, God of my master Abraham, give me success today, and show kindness to my master Abraham. See, I am standing beside this spring, and the daughters of the townspeople are coming out to draw water. May it be that when I say to a girl, 'Please let down your jar that I may have a drink,' and she says, 'Drink, and I'll water your camels too'—let her be the one you have chosen for your servant Isaac. By this I will know that you have shown kindness to my master."

Before he had finished praying, Rebekah came out with her jar on her shoulder. She was the daughter of Bethuel son of Milcah, who was the wife of Abraham's brother Nahor. The girl was very beautiful, a virgin; no man had

ever lain with her. She went down to the spring, filled her jar and came up again.

The servant hurried to meet her and said, "Please give me a little water from your jar."

"Drink, my lord," she said, and quickly lowered the jar to her hands and gave him a drink.

After she had given him a drink, she said, "I'll draw water for your camels too, until they have finished drinking." So she quickly emptied her jar into the trough, ran back to the well to draw more water, and drew enough for all his camels. Without saying a word, the man watched her closely to learn whether or not the Lord had made his journey successful.

When the camels had finished drinking, the man took out a gold nose ring weighing a beka and two gold bracelets weighing ten shekels. Then he asked, "Whose daughter are you? Please tell me, is there room in your father's house for us to spend the night?" . . .

Then the man bowed down and worshiped the Lord, saying, "Praise be to the Lord, the God of my master Abraham, who has not abandoned his kindness and faithfulness to my master. As for me, the Lord has led me on the journey to the house of my master's relatives."

The girl ran and told her mother's household about these things. Now Rebekah had a brother named Laban, and he hurried out to the man at the spring. . . .

So the man went to the house, and the camels were unloaded. Straw and fodder were brought for the camels, and water for him and his men to wash their feet. Then food was set before him, but he said, "I will not eat until I have told you what I have to say."

"Then tell us," Laban said. . . .

Laban and Bethuel answered, "This is from the Lord; we can say nothing to you one way or the other. Here is Rebekah; take her and go, and let her become the wife of your master's son, as the Lord has directed."

When Abraham's servant heard what they said, he bowed down to the ground before the Lord. . . .

Then Rebekah and her maids got ready and mounted their camels and went back with the man. . . .

Then the servant told Isaac all he had done. Isaac brought her into the tent of his mother Sarah, and he married Rebekah. So she became his wife, and he loved her; and Isaac was comforted after his mother's death. . . .

This is the account of Abraham's son Isaac. Abraham became the father of Isaac, and Isaac was forty years old when he married Rebekah daughter of Bethuel the Aramean from Paddan Aram and sister of Laban the Aramean.

Isaac prayed to the Lord on behalf of his wife, because she was barren. The Lord answered his prayer, and his wife Rebekah became pregnant.

1. Go through the text and underline any phrases or words that help you understand what's going on. Put a question mark next to anything you don't understand.

2. In the space below, write down some of your observations about Abraham. Based on your observations, do you think God has kept His promise to Abraham?

3. As usual, divide the text into scenes and give each scene a title. In the margins, list, in order of appearance, the main characters in the drama.

4. Fill in the chart again, and be sure to include some other themes you discovered in the text.

God	People	God—People	People—People	Other Themes

5. In the space below, write which characters have the starring roles. Who's the supporting cast? Did anyone get overlooked? If so, why?

6. At the beginning of the text, Abraham gives instructions to his servant. The servant questions the plan's success. Put Abraham's response in your own words. Describe the role God plays in Abraham's marriage plans for Isaac. Does this give you any insight into Abraham's faith? Explain.

7. Mark in the text where prayer is mentioned in one form or another. How did prayer influence God, people, and situations? Write down some things you discover about prayer in this text.

8. List the transition points in Abraham's life. The end of the text that's reprinted on page 94 is actually a transition point in chapter 25, but it does describe Isaac and Rebekah's early life together. Based on this, how has God's promise to Abraham been passed on to Isaac?

9. Do you think God has a design or plan for your life? Why or why not? If you think He does, write down some ways He is working to bring about His plans for you.

PRAYER PERSONAL

He who dwells in the shelter of the Most High will rest in the shadow of the Almighty. I will say of the Lord, "He is my refuge and my fortress, my God, in whom I trust." Psalm 91:1, 2

It's easy to get bogged down and feel anxious about everything in life. But the reality is that God is working on your behalf. He can help you jump over the obstacles, and to trust Him and His plans for you.

Finish this prayer, and then pray it aloud to the God of Abraham and Isaac—and look what He did for those guys.

Lord, as I think about Your plan for me, thank You for already showing me these things about Your design for me . . .

But I'm afraid these things are keeping me from trusting You and Your plan for me . . .

Birth-Order Blues
GENESIS 25; 27

Under each heading below list the things you feel are messed up about your life—past or present.

Relationships	Home Life	Attitudes	Parents	School

God works out His plans despite imperfect people, damaged emotions, failing relationships, and tons of other "human" disorders. Isaac and his family are the classic example of this, especially when Isaac's two sons get hit with the birth-order blues. For the complete story of Jacob and Esau, check out Genesis 25—33. You might be surprise at what you read in the Bible.

Read the following portions of Genesis 25 and 27.

Isaac prayed to the Lord on behalf of his wife, because she was barren. The Lord answered his prayer, and his wife Rebekah became pregnant. The babies jostled each other within her, and she said, "Why is this happening to me?" So she went to inquire of the Lord.

The Lord said to her,"Two nations are in your womb, and two peoples from within you will be separated; one people will be stronger than the other,

and the older will serve the younger."

When the time came for her to give birth, there were twin boys in her womb. The first to come out was red, and his whole body was like a hairy garment; so they named him Esau. After this, his brother came out, with his hand grasping Esau's heel; so he was named Jacob. Isaac was sixty years old when Rebekah gave birth to them.

The boys grew up, and Esau became a skillful hunter, a man of the open country, while Jacob was a quiet man, staying among the tents. Isaac, who had a taste for wild game, loved Esau, but Rebekah loved Jacob.

Once when Jacob was cooking some stew, Esau came in from the open country, famished. He said to Jacob, "Quick, let me have some of that red stew! I'm famished!" (That is why he was also called Edom.)

Jacob replied, "First sell me your birthright."

"Look, I am about to die," Esau said. "What good is the birthright to me?"

But Jacob said, "Swear to me first." So he swore an oath to him, selling his birthright to Jacob.

Then Jacob gave Esau some bread and some lentil stew. He ate and drank, and then got up and left.

So Esau despised his birthright. . . .

When Isaac was old and his eyes were so weak that he could no longer see, he called for Esau his older son and said to him, "My son."

"Here I am," he answered.

Isaac said, "I am now an old man and don't know the day of my death. Now then, get your weapons—your quiver and bow—and go out to the open country to hunt some wild game for me. Prepare me the kind of tasty food I like and bring it to me to eat, so that I may give you my blessing before I die."

Now Rebekah was listening as Isaac spoke to his son Esau. When Esau left for the open country to hunt game and bring it back, Rebekah said to her son Jacob, "Look, I overheard your father say to your brother Esau, 'Bring me some game and prepare me some tasty food to eat, so that I may give you my blessing in the presence of the Lord before I die.' Now, my son, listen carefully and do what I tell you: Go out to the flock and bring me two choice young goats, so I can prepare some tasty food for your father, just the way he likes it. Then take it to your father to eat, so that he may give you his blessing before he dies." . . .

So he went and got them and brought them to his mother, and she prepared some tasty food, just the way his father liked it. Then Rebekah took the best clothes of Esau her older son, which she had in the house, and put them on her younger son Jacob. She also covered his hands and the smooth part of his neck with the goatskins. Then she handed to her son Jacob the tasty food and the bread she had made.

He went to his father and said, "My father."

"Yes, my son," he answered. "Who is it?"

Jacob said to his father, "I am Esau your firstborn. I have done as you told me. Please sit up and eat some of my game so that you may give me your blessing." . . .

Then Isaac said to Jacob, "Come near so I can touch you, my son, to know whether you really are my son Esau or not."

Jacob went close to his father Isaac, who touched him and said, "The voice is the voice of Jacob, but the hands are the hands of Esau." He did not recognize him, for his hands were hairy like those of his brother Esau; so he blessed him. "Are you really my son Esau?" he asked.

"I am," he replied.

Then he said, "My son, bring me some of your game to eat, so that I may give you my blessing."

Jacob brought it to him and he ate; and he brought some wine and he drank. Then his father Isaac said to him, "Come here, my son, and kiss me."

So he went to him and kissed him. When Isaac caught the smell of his clothes, he blessed him. . . .

After Isaac finished blessing him and Jacob had scarcely left his father's presence, his brother Esau came in from hunting. He too prepared some tasty food and brought it to his father. Then he said to him, "My father, sit up and eat some of my game, so that you may give me your blessing."

His father Isaac asked him, "Who are you?"

"I am your son," he answered, "your firstborn, Esau."

Isaac trembled violently and said, "Who was it, then, that hunted game and brought it to me? I ate it just before you came and I blessed him—and indeed he will be blessed!"

When Esau heard his father's words, he burst out with a loud and bitter cry and said to his father, "Bless me—me too, my father!"

But he said, "Your brother came deceitfully and took your blessing."

Esau said, "Isn't he rightly named Jacob? He has deceived me these two times: He took my birthright, and now he's taken my blessing!" Then he asked, "Haven't you reserved any blessing for me?"

Isaac answered Esau, "I have made him lord over you and have made all his relatives his servants, and I have sustained him with grain and new wine. So what can I possibly do for you, my son?" . . .

Esau held a grudge against Jacob because of the blessing his father had given him. He said to himself, "The days of mourning for my father are near; then I will kill my brother Jacob."

When Rebekah was told what her older son Esau had said, she sent for her younger son Jacob and said to him, "Your brother Esau is consoling himself with the thought of killing you. Now then, my son, do what I say: Flee at once to my brother Laban in Haran. Stay with him for a while until your brother's fury subsides. When your brother is no longer angry with you and forgets what you did to him, I'll send word for you to come back from there. Why should I lose both of you in one day?" . . .

1. Reread the text. Describe your first impression of Isaac and his family. What's your first impression of this story?

2. Talk about a dysfunctional family! Go back through the text, and analyze each person's motives, character flaws, and the effect or problems all this created in this family. Record your discoveries on the chart below.

Name	Motives	Character Flaws	Problems

3. Describe the emotions (or clues to emotions) you discover in the story. Suppose Isaac, Rebekah, Jacob, and Esau had gathered in the family room for the evening. Draw where you think each person would sit, and explain why.

4. God has a mostly silent but constant role in the story. Go back through the text, and in the space below, write the times you see the effect of God's proclamation that "the older will serve the younger" (Genesis 25:23).

5. Do you think it was fair or unfair that Jacob received the blessing instead of Esau? Support your position from the text.

6. Isaac and Rebekah were almost as manipulating as their sons. List the times you think Isaac and Rebekah were dishonest and manipulative. Why do you think God allowed His promised heir to act like this?

7. From your perspective what things are messed up in your family relationships? How do you think God views those things? How do you think He could work with, or in spite of, those problems? Write down some of your thoughts to these questions.

8. From what you've studied this week, what have you discovered about your relationship with God? about your level of trust in Him? Circle the level that best describes you right now, and explain why.

HIGH

MEDIUM

LOW

PRAYER
PERSONAL

How great is the love the Father has lavished on us, that we should be called children of God! I John 3:1a

God has unshakable plans for His children. As you trust God, He'll unfold His grand design for your life. You don't have to struggle for power or position as long as you depend on God.

Lord, here are the things I want to be a part of my future . . .

When I think about trusting You with my dreams and plans, I feel . . .

Help me trust You in these situations . . .

and not to blame the situations or people.
Thank You . . .

Amazing Technicolor Trust, Part I

GENESIS 37; 39; 40

Life is difficult. Draw a graph of one of your most difficult periods. Chart your ups and downs, and write in any emotions you remember feeling at the time (anger, frustration, apathy, hope).

Starting Point   Ending Point

About a third of the Book of Genesis is devoted to Joseph. His story is pretty fantastic, with or without Andrew Lloyd Webber's musical, "Joseph and the Amazing Technicolor Dreamcoat." Joseph might seem larger than life at times, but he can show you how to handle the difficult stuff of life.

Read Genesis 37:1-8; 39:1-6; 40:14, 15, 23.

(You'll definitely need your Bible too.)

Jacob lived in the land where his father had stayed, the land of Canaan.

This is the account of Jacob.

Joseph, a young man of seventeen, was tending the flocks with his brothers, the sons of Bilhah and the sons of Zilpah, his father's wives, and he brought their father a bad report about them.

Now Israel [Jacob] loved Joseph more than any of his other sons, because he had been born to him in his old age; and he made a richly ornamented robe for him. When his brothers saw that their father loved him more than any of them, they hated him and could not speak a kind word to him.

Joseph had a dream, and when he told it to his brothers, they hated him all the more. He said to them, "Listen to this dream I had: We were binding sheaves of grain out in the field when suddenly my sheaf rose and stood upright, while your sheaves gathered around mine and bowed down to it."

His brothers said to him (fill in what you think his brothers said),

_____

*   *   *

Now Joseph had been taken down to Egypt. Potiphar, an Egyptian who was one of Pharaoh's officials, the captain of the guard, bought him from the Ishmaelites who had taken him there.

The Lord was with Joseph and he prospered, and he lived in the house of his Egyptian master. When his master saw that the Lord was with him and that the Lord gave him success in everything he did, Joseph found favor in his eyes and became his attendant. Potiphar put him in charge of his household, and he entrusted to his care everything he owned. From the time he put him in charge of his household and of all that he owned, the Lord blessed the household of the Egyptian because of Joseph. The blessing of the Lord was on everything Potiphar had, both in the house and in the field. So he left in Joseph's care everything he had; with Joseph in charge, he did not concern himself with anything except the food he ate.

Now Joseph was well-built and handsome. . . .

[At this point, Joseph's story takes on a soap opera-like quality. Potiphar's wife made several passes at Joseph, Joseph turned her down each time, and she framed Joseph. The next thing you know, Potiphar put Joseph in prison. Check out Genesis 39. We pick up the Scripture in Genesis 40, where Joseph is in prison and interpreting dreams.]

*   *   *

"But when all goes well with you, remember me and show me kindness; mention me to Pharaoh and get me out of this prison. For I was forcibly carried off from the land of the Hebrews, and even here I have done nothing to deserve being put in a dungeon." . . .

The chief cupbearer, however, did not remember Joseph; he forgot him.

1. Look up Genesis 37:8 in your Bible to see how Joseph's brothers reacted to his dream. How did your reaction compare with theirs? Do you think their reaction was justified? Why or why not?

2. Skim all of chapter 37, and list all the actual problems and potential for problems in this family.

3. Using the information in Genesis 37 and 39, describe Joseph. (It's okay if you leave some categories blank.)

Physically	Spiritually	Morally	Emotionally

4. Now describe the brothers—especially the problems they had with Joseph, as well as their emotional state.

5. Write down some things that bother you about Joseph.

6. Based on Genesis 37, 39, and 40, chart out Joseph's ups and downs. Fill in the highlights, and low-lights, of his life. Also, jot down Joseph's attitude at different times in his life.

Starting Point   Ending Point

7. Look through these three chapters again, and come up with a constant theme. Why did you choose this theme, and what does it tell you about God and Joseph?

8. We're sort of leaving Joseph hanging in midair, so what advice would you give him and why?

He provides food for those who fear him; he remembers his covenant forever. He has shown his people the power of his works, giving them the lands of other nations. . . . He provided redemption for his people; he ordained his covenant forever—holy and awesome is his name. Psalm 111:5, 6, 9

Sometimes we need to take another look at our situation, refocus our attention, and realize that God is with us. Take a couple of minutes to look at some of the prayers you wrote in this journal, and then finish this prayer of thanksgiving.

God, looking back, I can tell that You were with me when . . .

Thank You for . . .

Amazing Technicolor Trust, Part II

GENESIS 41—45

Everyone has different reactions to major disappointments. Complete these thoughts.

• Things in my life that have been major disappointments include . . .

AND THE MAJOR DISAPPOINTMENT GOES TO . . .

• Here are some ways I react to bad news or disappointments . . .

• These things help me get a perspective on the situation . . .

Of course, there's a sequel to Joseph's story. After all, we purposely left him in prison—forgotten by all. This week, Joseph is on the move again as he trusts God and His plan.

Read Genesis 41:9-14, 41-43; 42:21-24; 45:1-8.

(You'll need your Bible in order to cruise through Genesis 41—45; 50, stopping here and there to look at specific passages.)

Then the chief cupbearer said to Pharaoh, "Today I am reminded of my shortcomings. Pharaoh was once angry with his servants, and he imprisoned me and the chief baker in the house of the captain of the guard. Each of us had a dream the same night, and each dream had a meaning of its own. Now a young Hebrew was there with us, a servant of the captain of the guard. We told him our dreams, and he interpreted them for us, giving each man the interpretation of his dream. And things turned out exactly as he interpreted them to us: I was restored to my position, and the other man was hanged."

So Pharaoh sent for Joseph, and he was quickly brought from the dungeon. When he had shaved and changed his clothes, he came before Pharaoh.

*　　*　　*

So Pharaoh said to Joseph, "I hereby put you in charge of the whole land of Egypt." Then Pharaoh took his signet ring from his finger and put it on Joseph's finger. He dressed him in robes of fine linen and put a gold chain around his neck. He had him ride in a chariot as his second-in-command, and men shouted before him, "Make way!" Thus he put him in charge of the whole land of Egypt.

*　　*　　*

[Joseph's brothers] They said to one another, "Surely we are being punished because of our brother. We saw how distressed he was when he pleaded with us for his life, but we would not listen; that's why this distress has come upon us."

Reuben replied, "Didn't I tell you not to sin against the boy? But you wouldn't listen! Now we must give an accounting for his blood." They did not realize that Joseph could understand them, since he was using an interpreter.

He turned away from them and began to weep, but then turned back and spoke to them again. He had Simeon taken from them and bound before their eyes.

*　　　*　　　*

Then Joseph could no longer control himself before all his attendants, and he cried out, "Have everyone leave my presence!" So there was no one with Joseph when he made himself known to his brothers. And he wept so loudly that the Egyptians heard him, and Pharaoh's household heard about it.

Joseph said to his brothers, "I am Joseph! Is my father still living?" But his brothers were not able to answer him, because they were terrified at his presence.

Then Joseph said to his brothers, "Come close to me." When they had done so, he said, "I am your brother Joseph, the one you sold into Egypt! And now, do not be distressed and do not be angry with yourselves for selling me here, because it was to save lives that God sent me ahead of you. For two years now there has been famine in the land, and for the next five years there will not be plowing and reaping. But God sent me ahead of you to preserve for you a remnant on earth and to save your lives by a great deliverance.

"So then, it was not you who sent me here, but God. He made me father to Pharaoh, lord of his entire household and ruler of all Egypt."

1. How would you react if people shouted, "Make way!" whenever you walked by? How do you think you'd handle power if it were handed to you as it was handed to Joseph?

2. Skim Genesis 41 and compare Pharaoh's perspective on the situation with Joseph's perspective. (Also check out the last two paragraphs of the Scripture printed on page 114.) How do you think this affected Joseph's attitude once he had all this power?

3. Stop and read Genesis 42:6, 7 in your Bible. Remind you of anything? If so, what? Why do you think Joseph acted the way he did?

4. Do a quick read of Genesis 43 and 44 and the third section of Scripture printed on pages 114, 115. Describe how Joseph's brothers are feeling about what they did to him. Play the psychologist and speculate at some of the problems their guilt may have caused the family.

5. In the text, underline Joseph's emotions. You might also want to read Genesis 43:30, 31. What does this tell you about Joseph's attitude toward his brothers?

6. Why do you think Joseph didn't jump at the chance to get even with his brothers? Hint: Think about the major assumption Joseph was operating on.

7. Check out Genesis 45:14, 15; 50:15-21. In your own words, explain how this long family conflict was finally resolved. Do you think it was a good resolution to the family's problems? Why or why not?

8. Go back and reread some of the stuff you wrote in your journal about God's relationship with people, and their relationship with Him. In the space below, write down a couple of your major discoveries about

• God's relationship with the people He created

• People's relationship with the God who created them

• Your relationship with God

PRAYER PERSONAL

He has caused his wonders to be remembered; the Lord is gracious and compassionate. Psalm 111:4

If there's one thing you should have figured out from this trek through the Book of Genesis it is that God is personally involved with His creation. How does that make you feel?

Take a few minutes to express your feelings, fears, and thanks to the very personal God of creation.